STRATEGIC
STUDIES
INSTITUTE

The Strategic Studies Institute (SSI) is part of the U.S. Army War College and is the strategic-level study agent for issues related to national security and military strategy with emphasis on geostrategic analysis.

The mission of SSI is to use independent analysis to conduct strategic studies that develop policy recommendations on:

- Strategy, planning, and policy for joint and combined employment of military forces;

- Regional strategic appraisals;

- The nature of land warfare;

- Matters affecting the Army's future;

- The concepts, philosophy, and theory of strategy; and,

- Other issues of importance to the leadership of the Army.

Studies produced by civilian and military analysts concern topics having strategic implications for the Army, the Department of Defense, and the larger national security community.

In addition to its studies, SSI publishes special reports on topics of special or immediate interest. These include edited proceedings of conferences and topically oriented roundtables, expanded trip reports, and quick-reaction responses to senior Army leaders.

The Institute provides a valuable analytical capability within the Army to address strategic and other issues in support of Army participation in national security policy formulation.

Strategic Studies Institute
and
U.S. Army War College Press

AFTER THE SPRING:
REFORMING ARAB ARMIES

Florence Gaub

September 2014

*****

Comments pertaining to this report are invited and should be forwarded to: Director, Strategic Studies Institute and U.S. Army War College Press, U.S. Army War College, 47 Ashburn Drive, Carlisle, PA 17013-5010.

*****

This manuscript was funded by the U.S. Army War College External Research Associates Program. Information on this program is available on our website, *www.StrategicStudies Institute.army.mil*, at the Opportunities tab.

*****

*****

The Strategic Studies Institute and U.S. Army War College Press publishes a monthly email newsletter to update the national security community on the research of our analysts, recent and forthcoming publications, and upcoming conferences sponsored by the Institute. Each newsletter also provides a strategic commentary by one of our research analysts. If you are interested in receiving this newsletter, please subscribe on the SSI website at *www.StrategicStudiesInstitute.army.mil/newsletter*.

FOREWORD

Although Arab military forces had somewhat disappeared from the political landscape since the 1970s, the events of the "Arab Spring" in 2011 have brought them back to the forefront of political change, for better or for worse. Not only were all the challenged regimes of military background, i.e., in Tunisia, Egypt, Libya, Syria, and Yemen, but the armed forces played a decisive role in the fall or maintenance of the regimes in question.

The future of these forces is therefore crucial in a continuing time of often turbulent change in the Arab world. Outsiders, such as the United States, are challenged to go beyond classical security sector assistance and instead rethink the security sector in these states in a more holistic and comprehensive manner.

As Dr. Florence Gaub shows in this compelling monograph, seven areas are of particular concern when addressing the reform of Arab military forces and their domestic counterparts. Ranging from over-politicization to financial constraints, the task to reform might be huge but is not unmanageable. Although the ongoing security challenges may invite postponement of reform until a more suitable moment, the time to reform is now more than ever.

As the Arab world navigates this difficult time of transition, the capacity of its external and internal security sectors to reform themselves will be crucial in the outcome of this challenging journey.

DOUGLAS C. LOVELACE, JR.
Director
Strategic Studies Institute and
U.S. Army War College Press

ABOUT THE AUTHOR

FLORENCE GAUB is a Senior Analyst at the European Union Institute for Security Studies where she heads the Middle East/Mediterranean program. She works on the Arab world with a focus on strategy and security. In addition to monitoring post-conflict developments in Iraq, Lebanon, and Libya, she works on Arab military forces, conflict structures, geostrategic dimensions of the Arab region, and intercultural communication. She was previously assigned to the North Atlantic Treaty Organization (NATO) Defence College and the German parliament. Dr. Gaub has published several articles and two books on these topics, and has lectured widely with European governments, the NATO school at Oberammergau, Joint Forces Command Naples, and several think tanks and universities in the Middle East, Europe and the United States. Dr. Gaub holds degrees from Sciences Po Paris, Sorbonne, and Munich universities. She holds a Ph.D. from Humboldt University Berlin, where she wrote her thesis on the Lebanese army.

SUMMARY

The Arab Spring had a military dimension in both its targets — regimes with a military background — and its outcomes. Where the armed forces in their entirety or partially sided with the protesters regime change succeeded; where they did not, it failed.

The somewhat renewed political role of Arab forces has therefore underlined not only their importance, but also the necessity for reform. This monograph focuses on the structural aspects of reform that would benefit the Arab Spring forces; it identifies seven features which need to be addressed when attempting Arab military reform in the countries affected by large-scale unrest in 2011. These are: an unclear mandate, over-politicization, lack of civilian oversight, a challenging ongoing security situation, limited resources, pockets of paramilitary activity, and, in parts, lack of an institutional perception of the need to reform. It looks at the reasons for these features and formulates possible solutions.

Generally speaking, Arab military forces operate in a very difficult environment on several accounts. usually part of state systems which emerged only in the 20th century, they are tied to weak states in terms of sovereignty but also in terms of legitimacy; they are also challenged geographically and militarily; and often suffer from lack of funding either due to economic constraints or deliberate shortage by the regime which seeks to keep the military weak. Institutionally, Arab armed forces need not only internal reform but would also benefit greatly from greater regional integration, stabilization, and the resolution of ongoing conflicts. Arab military forces need political neutralization in a benign (rather than malign) manner, such as fully professional and meritocratic recruitment and promotion criteria, educational curricula emphasizing the subordination of the armed forces to civilian control, clear separation of internal and external security tasks, and a spelled out national security strategy streamlining the military's efforts.

It is important to involve the security sector agents themselves in the process to overcome institutional opposition; appealing to professional ethics and identity is equally bound to be more successful than patronizing civilian attitudes. Ultimately, security sector reform against the wishes of the sector in question will always result in mitigated success, if not to say failure.

For better or for worse, Arab security sectors remain one of the pillars of Arab states. Without security, no economic development is possible in either Libya or Egypt—and economic conditions led to the 2011 events in the first place. Western governments so far have refrained from extensive security sector reform in the Arab world, preferring security sector assistance or occasional training. What 2011 has shown, however, is that reforms are not only beneficial, but at this stage mandatory. Since civilian actors are themselves challenged by ongoing transitions, the main agents in this reform will have to be the institutions themselves. Understanding their concerns and needs will certainly foster their cooperation—and in any case such understanding is crucial to delivering the efficient and legally bound security sector that citizens and institutions alike are striving for.

AFTER THE SPRING:
REFORMING ARAB ARMIES

The Arab Spring was widely hailed as a popular uprising against authoritarian dictatorships; but it also had a military dimension in both the protests' targets and the role of the armed forces in facilitating, or obstructing, regime change. All the challenged regimes had a military background — Tunisia's President Zine El Abidine Ben Ali, a former air force officer, seized power in 1987 with the help of two fellow graduates from the French military academy Saint-Cyr; Yemen's President Ali Abdullah Saleh was an army officer turned military governor who became president, chief of staff and commander in chief in 1978; Egypt's President Hosni Mubarak, previously commander of the nation's air force and a trained fighter pilot, took over from President Anwar Sadat (himself an army officer) following his assassination in 1981; Libya's Colonel Muammar Gaddafi came to power in a 1969 military coup; and Syria's President Bashar al-Assad's father Hafez, from whom he inherited the rule, had risen to power from the air force's ranks.

Because the regimes had come to power and consolidated themselves by military means, the armed forces were seen as part and parcel of the systems, loyal to the rulers, and integral parts of a system of repression. In two of the countries, Egypt and Tunisia, the military forces joined the demonstrators; in two, Libya and Yemen, they disintegrated in the face of popular protest; and in only one, Syria, did the military forces stand (and continue to stand) firmly with the regime.

It has been explained elsewhere how these actions depended in large part on the internal state of the

1

armed forces and their reduced, or adequate, military capabilities[1]; this monograph, however, seeks to assess the challenges these forces are facing when it comes to reform in the near- and mid-term future. It focuses on the five countries of the Arab Spring (Tunisia, Egypt, Libya, Yemen, and, to some extent, Syria), but lessons drawn here are applicable to other Arab states as well, and it prioritizes the armed forces over the police, although similar features are present there as well.

Although security sector **assistance** has been granted to these states by several outside actors ranging from the United States to Europe and international organizations in the last decades, security sector **reform** (SSR) is more comprehensive and holistic. The Arab security sectors affected by the Arab Spring are also the ones that require SSR the most; not only because they are in a particularly challenging situation of transition, but also because their condition has contributed to the Arab Spring.

What Is Security Sector Reform?

Born in 1998, SSR is a concept which introduces two criteria to assess the effectiveness and efficiency of a given sector. These are the professional delivery of security to individual citizens and civilian control or accountability. Although often seen primarily as the attempt to install human rights protection into the sector in question, SSR is also about professionalization of the armed forces in order to improve the delivery of security to the people.

In an ideal world, the security sector has laws and doctrines explaining its task, its mandate, and its purpose; a sector which knows what to do how to do it and why — in other words, is professional. It is controlled by certain elements of the state and society, and is subject to codified law. In a triangle of state, people, and security sector, the former, accountable to its people, controls the latter so that it delivers security to its people. In the Arab world, this is often upside down: Nobody is accountable to the people, and therefore the state controls the country, often violently. At the same time, the state generally does not trust the armed forces and therefore makes sure that they underperform in order to not become a political threat. In other words, the system is upside down; changing it means changing the whole system; the people, rather than being the object of security, have to become its subject.

This monograph focuses on the structural aspects of reform the Arab Spring forces would benefit from; it identifies seven features which need to be addressed when attempting Arab military reform in the countries affected by large-scale unrest in 2011: 1) an unclear mandate, 2) over-politicization, 3) lack of civilian oversight, 4) a challenging ongoing security situation, 5) limited resources, 6) pockets of paramilitary activity, and, in parts, 7) the lack of an institutional perception of the need to reform. Arab military forces generally operate in a very difficult environment on several accounts: usually part of state systems which emerged only in the 20th century, they are tied to weak states in terms of sovereignty but also in terms of legitimacy; they are also challenged geographically and militarily; and often suffer from lack of funding either due to economic constraints or deliberate shortage of resources by the regime which seeks to keep the military weak. Institutionally, Arab armed forces need not only internal reform but would also benefit greatly from greater regional integration, stabilization, and the resolution of ongoing conflicts.

An Unclear Mandate.

The security concerns perceived by a given state, and proposed attempts to counter them, are laid out in many states in a national security strategy, also called a white paper on defense or security. It is generally developed by the executive branch of government periodically to streamline decisions pertaining to training, weapons procurements, recruitment, and the development of strategies of different security branches. Although not a *sine qua non* for national defense, such a document proves useful when several different agencies have to cooperate in a very complex field.

Surprisingly, the majority of Arab states — examples include Tunisia, Egypt, Algeria, and Yemen — do not have such a nationally defined security strategy. More recently, Lebanon, Iraq, and Libya developed one only after major internal conflict. In several states, strategy is confused with doctrine which defines a standard set of maneuvers, kinds of troops, and weapons which are employed as a default approach to some anticipated kind of attack. Strategy, as opposed to doctrine, defines an overarching plan to achieve one or more goals under conditions of uncertainty.

There are a number of reasons for the lack of such a basic yet crucial document: The pronounced opacity of the defense sector in these states has made national or even institutional informed debates on strategy and security almost impossible; national defense is considered the prerogative of the head of state only, with the possible advice of the military's highest echelons, making a national document unnecessary (or seen as unnecessary); finally, the defense posture of most Arab states has focused over decades only on Israel in spite of strategic evolutions and the fact that the man-power intensive wars of 1948, 1967, and 1973 did not achieve the desired result. Although ossified, this stance suited the political narrative and prevented an evolutionary debate on defense and security.

The absence of such a document has not only several reasons, it also has crucial consequences: inefficient spending of an already limited defense budget, inadequate training and leadership conceptualization, doctrines detached from strategic goals, and incoherent prioritization of resources and personnel, to name just a few. Where a national strategy is nonexistent, it is logically also not reviewed regularly, and, as a consequence, a generalized process of renewal does not take place — or if it does, it does not do so as a result of strategic considerations, but of logistical or political ones. The Egyptian switch from Soviet to American doctrine in the late-1970s, for instance, was not triggered by a renewal in strategic thinking (although the return of the Sinai to Egyptian control was indeed the result of Sadat's improved strategic assessment).[2] This is not to say that the mentioned states do not have a strategy — but they do not have a basic document available to all, the result of an institutional debate serving as a guiding star in all decisions pertaining to national security and defense.

This blurring of purpose is found not only in matters of national defense; it exists at the security level at large. More often than not, Arab military forces take on internal security tasks. This is the result of a horizontal rather than vertical division of labor between external and internal security forces; a hierarchy in which the armed forces usually rank above the other security agencies. Unclear responsibilities, preferential political treatment, uneven resources and lack of distinction between security agencies lead to idiosyncratic and convoluted security structures. Reflected in the resemblance of police and military uniforms, the armed forces often take on internal security tasks ranging from securing of elections to riot control.

This vague purpose of existence, mission, and tasks across different agencies has a negative effect not only on the armed forces, but on all actors in the security sector; a starting point for reform therefore would be the establishment of key documents such as a national security strategy as well as mission statements for the security agencies in charge of its execution, including the military.

Over-Politicization.

Arab armed forces have more often than not played a political role since independence; coups d'etat — here defined as a forceful seizure of executive authority and office by a dissident/opposition faction with the support/impetus of military officers, (excluding revolutions, victories by oppositional forces in civil wars, popular uprisings, and palace coups) are a frequent feature in the Arab world.

Since the first coup occurred in 1936 in newly sovereign Iraq, almost 60 military attempts at political interference have taken place, half of them successful. Syria and Iraq were particularly prone to them (17 attempts in the first case, 11 in the second), contrary to the commonly held belief that coups are less frequent in plural societies since officers would struggle to build cross-communitarian alliances.[3] Although it is true that the phenomenon has died down somewhat since the 1980s — most coups have taken place in the three decades following World War II — it is still not extinct: Successful coups in Sudan in 1989, Algeria in 1992, Mauritania in 2008, and in Egypt in 2013 (not to mention four failed attempts in Iraq, Sudan, and Mauritania between 1990 and 2008) remind us that Arab armed forces still do play a political role.

Coup frequency, however, is not a reliable indicator for military involvement in politics; absence of military coup attempts, such as in Syria since 1982, might simply indicate that the regime has managed to consolidate itself by co-opting the armed forces into its system. It is worth noting that military coups occur more often in republican systems — this is less so because monarchies do not attract military meddling, but rather because coups take place more often in states in which they have already occurred. Simply put, military coups attract more military coups. Monarchies such as Jordan, Morocco, Libya (until 1969), and Iraq (until 1958) have indeed experienced such attempts, also; but whereas the first two managed to contain the threat, the latter two did not. In contrast to this, the Gulf States, by and large, have not seen any military interference with their politics.

Events since 2011 have indeed shown that the Arab armed forces are still very much involved in their national politics; the Yemeni as well as Tunisian military facilitated regime-change by siding with the protesters; Egypt's armed forces helped oust first an autocrat and then an elected president; and the Syrian armed forces are fighting a domestic war against their own people on behalf of the regime. In Lebanon, a former officer is leaving the presidential palace only to be replaced by another; and rumors of Tunisia's previous Chief of Staff running for president in late-2014 are already ripe.

There are several reasons for Arab military involvement in their country's politics; for a start, armed forces have coercive advantages they can use for political means, but in many Arab states they are also un-checked by the civilian regime. Weak states and governments, largely the outcome of unconsolidated sovereignty and lack of resources, are easy targets for armed forces eager to get involved in politics.[4] It is therefore a combination of push- and pull-factors which lead to political involvement by the military.

The involvement of the armed forces in politics is a concern when it comes to SSR. It not only negatively affects the establishment and consolidation of democratic systems, but it equally has a detrimental effect on the armed forces' capacity. It distracts from the military's main purpose—defense of the nation—and thereby impedes cohesion, command and control structures, and leadership, and invites corruption into the military. The 1967 defeat of Egypt against Israel is an example of how the close intertwinement of military and politics will have a negative effect on strategic assessment, command, control, and leadership.[5]

Where the military is seen as a potential threat to the regime, the latter might even take purposeful measures to deliberately reduce the institution's coup capacity. A side effect of such "coup-proofing" measures is an immediate reduction in military professionalism and capability. A salient example is the Libyan military, which Colonel Qaddafi coup-proofed to the extent that it was of almost no use at all during the 2011 war.[6]

Removing the armed forces from politics is therefore in the professional interest of any military organization, but it is notoriously long to achieve—according to a World Bank study, it took the fastest 20 countries

17 years for achievement.[7] Successful measures to neutralize the military politically include fully professional and meritocratic recruitment and promotion criteria, educational curricula emphasizing the subordination of the armed forces to civilian control, clear separation of internal and external security tasks, and a spelled out national security strategy streamlining the military's efforts. Logically, these efforts never involve just the armed forces themselves, but are embedded in a broader political and social context.

Lack of Civilian Oversight.

Civilian oversight over the security sector in Arab countries is either nonexistent or mostly malign, rather than benign. More often than not, it consists of deliberate techniques aiming at weakening those aspects of the armed forces which could be used in a coup rather than ensuring its maximum professional capacity with a minimum of a political threat. Civilian oversight, as it is at its most effective, includes parliamentary oversight, transparent resource allocation, management of the defense sector, and clear legal as well as institutional frameworks. Most of these aspects are missing in the Arab world.

To begin with, some Arab parliaments (Morocco, Jordan, Oman, and Qatar) do not have a defense committee at all; in Tunisia, national defense was handled in parliament by the foreign affairs committee, but its powers were severely curtailed. It had no controlling rights over national defense industries and no say in the sending of troops abroad. Its function, rather than exerting civilian oversight over the armed forces, consisted in advising presidential national defense policies.

But even where a dedicated armed forces committee exists, its effective controlling mechanism is usually limited. This reflects of course these parliaments' limited role altogether, not just in matters pertaining to defense matters.

Things are slightly more intricate in Egypt, which has undergone several changes since the fall of Mubarak—none of which challenged the rather opaque control mechanisms over the armed forces.

In the 2012 constitution, defense was the matter of a subcommittee of the Committee on the System of Government. The 2014 constitution does not spell out the parliamentary committees, but it defines oversight of the executive as one of its tasks (which the 2012 constitution had not specified). Elsewhere, the military seems to control the civilians rather than the other way around: The Defense Minister, by law a military officer, needs to be approved by the Supreme Council of the Armed Forces, and civilians can be tried in military courts.[8] While parliament technically has full access and control over the state's budget, this does not apply to the defense budget which is overseen by a new body, the National Defense Council. Chaired by the President, it includes the Prime Minister, the Speaker of the House of Representatives, the Ministers of Defense, Foreign Affairs, Finance and Interior, the Chief of the General Intelligence Service, the Chief of Staff of the Armed Forces, the Commanders of the Navy, the Air Forces and Air Defense, the Chief of Operations of the Armed Forces, and the Head of Military Intelligence. Effectively, only six of its 14 members are civilians. According to the 2014 constitution, the council is "competent to discuss the budget of the Armed Forces, which shall be included in the State budget under one budget line."[9] This means that parliament will only see the total combined budget of the armed forces rather than a detailed breakdown, while control or even approval of the budget is not foreseen. On a more positive note, the President requires a two-thirds majority of the House of Representatives to declare war and send troops abroad.

Structures as the Egyptian one are rather common in Arab states; then again, the rather far-reaching measures of military self-protection against civilian interference do have a justified reason. Where institutions are weak and nepotism is frequent, decisionmaking structures pertaining to personnel, strategy development and even arms procurement are very vulnerable to political interference. This is particularly the case in highly hierarchical systems such as in the smaller Gulf States, where decisionmaking is highly personalized. Relevant bureaucracies, in particular defense ministries, therefore, need to be reformed along with the armed forces and be decoupled from the political level.

Finally, parliamentarians who have been elected in a fully democratic fashion frequently lack the experience and knowledge of how to fulfil their man date of oversight, and rarely have the adequate staff which could make up for this want. A case in point are the Libyan members of the General National Congress (GNC), who lacked clarity on the identity of the commander-in-chief, the role of the defense minister especially in relation to an overly active chief of staff, their own oversight role, and their available tools.[10] Inconsistencies in the institutional and legal context have seriously hampered Libya's reconstruction and has led to a high fluctuation in personnel: Chief of Staff Youssef al-Mangoush was removed by a vote of the GNC defense committee rather than the GNC as a whole, his differences with interim defense minister Osama al-Juwaili obstructed the drafting of Libya's White Paper; al-Juwaili's successor, Mohammed al-Barghati, had to resign at the same time as al-Mangoush, making way for Libya's third defense minister in 2 years, former military officer (and now prime minister) Abdullah Al-Thini.[11] Training is necessary to clarify the role of parliaments and of the different security agents, the available tools to exert control, and the existing legal frameworks.

More often than not, armed forces argue that the urgency of conflict and the necessity of secrecy in a time of war require limiting civilian interference with their affairs. Although it is true that the rather unique mission of the armed forces requires unique working conditions, this is not a valid argument in that it removes the armed forces effectively from any civilian control.

The Challenging Ongoing Security Situation.

A large majority of Arab countries are facing significant ongoing security challenges impeding reform efforts. These range from domestic turmoil to counterinsurgency, terrorism, civil war in Syria, and post-conflict insecurity features.

Egypt and Tunisia, for instance, have faced large-scale internal chaos since 2011, including mass demonstrations, riots, and arson. Egyptian security agents, largely untrained in crowd control and unequipped, have brutally repressed the masses. In the first wave of demonstrations in early-2011, at least 840 people were killed and 6,467 others were injured.[12] Almost 12,000 civilians were arrested and tried in military courts.[13] Throughout 2011 and 2012, protesters repeatedly clashed with security forces, resulting in several dead and injured. Between the coup in the summer of 2013 and the spring of 2014, more than 2,500 Egyptians have been killed, more than 17,000 wounded, and more than 16,000 arrested in demonstrations and clashes.[14] Undertaking reforms in such a context is arguably difficult, as the Egyptian Minister of Interior General Mohammed Ibrahim, put it:

> I have 186 dead officers and more than 800 injured so far, petty officers preventing security chiefs from entering offices, a presidential palace being torched on a weekly basis by a 100 or so kids, and Egypt's largest government complex was blocked for 4 days, so: when will I have time to reform? When these political polemics end.[15]

As security forces are overstretched, crime rates have gone up, too: Homicide rates have tripled since the 2011 uprising, kidnappings and car thefts have quadrupled, and armed robberies have increased 12-fold.[16] Under these circumstances, Egyptian police have gone on strike, protesting against their working conditions and the politicization of their work.[17]

In addition to this, terrorism is on the rise given the collapse of security agents in several Arab countries; terrorist attacks in Egypt, previously largely confined to the Sinai, have expanded throughout the country, claiming the lives of 281 Egyptians between July 2013 and January 2014, a 10-fold increase from the 28 victims during President Mohamed Morsi's year in office (July 2012-June 2013). Similarly, terrorism is on the rise in Tunisia, Libya, and Algeria; the terrorist attack on the Algerian gas facility in Amenas in early-2013 by an al-Qaeda affiliated group resulted in the death of 39 foreign hostages.

Libya in particular is facing severe post-conflict security challenges. It currently has over 150,000 militiamen on its streets, is awash with weapons and ammunition, and there is virtually no civilian oversight over the security sector. Police and armed forces largely melted away during the 2011 conflict and now need to be reconstructed amidst a very insecure and volatile environment.[18] While Libya turns into an almost lawless zone, its executive and legislative branches struggle with basic features of security sector reconstruction: 3 years after Qaddafi's demise, there is still no white paper on defense, no legal clarity on the post of commander-in-chief, and no agreed timeline for reforming security and integrating the militias, which now largely run the country. Frequent changes of ministers of interior and defense, as well as chiefs of staff, and an ongoing political vetting process have depleted the security sector of experienced personnel capable of implementing the necessary measures. In the absence of these, Libya has been unable to absorb the many assistance offers which were made by the United States as well as the European Union, its member states and the North Atlantic Treaty Organization. In contrast to Egypt or Tunisia, Libya's security institutions are not overstretched, they are simply not able to perform at all, given their lack of training and personnel. At the time of this writing, Libya had about 5,000 officers of colonel rank and just graduated its first batch of junior officers — there are virtually no middle rank officers and only a handful of junior ones.

The situation is complicated further by the fact that security institutions are now under attack by terrorists and angered civilians alike. In Libya, a targeted assassination campaign of security officials in the country's East has claimed at least 90 lives so far.[19] Vengeance attacks are also on the rise in Egypt, where a police headquarter was bombed in early 2014, and officers and soldiers have fallen victim to targeted assassinations.[20] In March 2014, Egyptian judges sentenced 529 people to death for attacking a police station, dragging out its chief officer and bludgeoning him to death.[21] Absenteeism, already significant before the uprisings, has grown sharply in Libya, with estimates ranging from 20 to 40 percent after officers were being harassed on the street by civilians.[22]

SSR, or reconstruction, is severely restricted by such conditions which limit time, resources, and personnel; where SSR has taken place successfully — most notably in Eastern Europe and the Balkans, security conditions were either stable enough, or security provisions were ensured by an external force. Neither is the case in those Arab countries facing the most pressing need for SSR.

Limited Resources.

At first sight, the Middle East and North Africa is a region dense in military spenders. Six of the global top 10 military spenders are located in the region: Oman (8.61 percent), Saudi Arabia (8 percent), Israel (5.7 percent), Jordan (4.6 percent), Algeria (4.5 percent), and Lebanon (4.1 percent) spend the equivalent or more than Russia and the United States (both 4.4. percent) in terms of gross domestic product (GDP) percentage, where the global average is 2.52 percent. In all cases, these states spend more on defense than on education and health.

But when taking into account the total amount of money spent on defense and security, a different picture presents itself. By and large, Arab security sectors operate in a highly resource restrained environment. In 2012, Tunisia spent U.S.$709 million, Yemen U.S.$1,439 million, Jordan U.S.$1,448 million, Lebanon U.S.$1,735 million, and Libya U.S.$2,987 million. Even Algeria, the top North African spender, with U.S.$9,325 million spent only a fraction of what Germany (U.S.$45,785 million), the United Kingdom (U.S.$60,840 million) or the United States (U.S.$682,478 million) spent. Egypt's military budget (U.S.$4,376 million) is a bit more difficult to assess given the large-scale economic activity the armed forces are engaged in and are not forced to disclose.[23]

Numbers are lower when it comes to internal security, although the events of 2011 have triggered higher spending in this domain. In Tunisia, the interior ministry's budget has increased to U.S.$86 million for 2014, to U.S.$3.3 billion in Egypt, and to U.S.$7.2 billion in Algeria.[24] Most of these added funds will go to personnel costs, either new positions (8,700 created in Tunisia) or salary increases and rewards for existing staff. This reflects spending on internal and external security more generally which is personnel-intensive rather than focused on weaponry or police equipment (with the notable exception of the Gulf States, which keep investing in modern technology).

But this spending is clouding a difficult financial reality. In Tunisia, the average police officer earns the equivalent of U.S.$250 — in comparison, a local bus driver or a lower-level bank employee earns more. In Egypt, lower-ranking police officers are paid some 800 Egyptian pounds — around U.S.$115 — per month.[25] In addition, internal security forces are over-burdened, often working a minimum of 12-hour shifts in areas as diverse as riot control, criminal investigation, traffic control, or monitoring of political opponents. Most judicial police are so underequipped that trials are based on witness accounts and confessions more than on evidence such as fingerprint analysis or DNA testing — or, in some cases as in Egypt there is no judicial police force at all. Those units conducting criminal investigation are limited not only in their executive powers but also in their resources.

The reason for this is that, with the exception of the Gulf States, most Arab states struggle financially. In North Africa and the Levant, economic performance has improved over the last decades, but it is still low: Egypt's per capita GDP is at U.S.$3,112 (in comparison, the American GDP per capita is at U.S.$49,922). High poverty rates, corruption, and low foreign direct investment result in underperforming institutions at all levels, including those in the security sector. What is worse, dysfunctional institutions and lack of security impede economic development significantly. According to the World Economic Forum, Egypt ranks 117 out of 148 when it comes to basic institutional requirements for competitiveness such as judicial independence, security, and the rule of law. It fared particularly badly with regards to the business costs of terrorism (148 out of 148), of crime and violence (143 out of 148), organized crime (138 out of 148), and reliability of police services (132 out of 148). Tunisia ranked somewhat higher, with 73 out of 148 when it comes to institutions, but like Egypt scored particularly badly on terrorism, organized crime, violence, and police reliability. Similar statistics exist for Algeria, Lebanon, Yemen, and Libya. Lebanon in particular has seen a direct impact of deteriorating security on its economy; its growth has been depressed to 0.9 percent in 2013, while the cumulative loss of GDP since the beginning of the crisis in 2011 stands now at U.S.$9.7 billion.[26] Of the non-Gulf Arab states, Jordan fared the best, ranking 28th out of 148 when it came to the reliability of its police forces, and 13th as well as 16th, respectively, with regard to organized crime and violence.

Simply put, Arab security sectors underperform in part due to harsh economic conditions, which in turn exist in part because the security sector underperforms. As a result, conditions for impending economic change are not ripe: Egypt, Algeria, Yemen, and Libya rank behind states such as Ghana or Jamaica in terms of competitiveness.[27] None of this applies to the Gulf states, which have managed to utilize their petroleum rents to further institution building; all of them fared well in categories such as police reliability, organized crime, and business costs of terrorism, with Qatar ranking amid the top three in every category related to institutions.

The case of Jordan, which ranks above European states such as France, Italy, or Portugal in terms of police reliability, proves, however, that resource constraints do not necessarily constitute an insurmountable obstacle to the establishment of security conditions conducive to economic development. Its GDP is at U.S.$4,879, which ranks below Lebanon (U.S.$10,311), Libya (U.S.$12,778) or Algeria (U.S.$5,694), and only slightly above Egypt and Tunisia—all states which score considerably worse than Jordan on security and institutional criteria.[28] This is not to say that Jordanian police are accountable, transparent, and respectful of human rights—in fact, they have been criticized for quite the opposite[29]—but they do support conditions for economic development. SSR therefore does not need to be obstructed solely by financial limits—but more often than not, includes side effects of low economic development; fuel shortages and other problems such as corruption, terrorism, and organized crime impede reform.

Pockets of Paramilitary Activity.

A significant number of Arab states have trouble asserting a monopoly of violence over their territory, which affects SSR considerably. Pockets of paramilitary activity hollow out not only existing provisions for civilian control and rule of law—since they operate outside the state system—they also disrupt other efforts related to SSR. Nonstate violence affects economic development even more than state-induced violence because it is less predictable; it weakens the state not only in its credibility, but is also a symptom of state weakness in the first place.

The most structured cases of paramilitary activity are Libya and Iraq; in Libya, up to 250,000 men are organized in militias which have emerged from the civil war in 2011. Worse, they have continued to proliferate once the conflict ended in the absence of state institutions. Over 300 of these groups, mostly clustered along regional lines, control security in areas as diverse as oil platforms and civilian neighborhoods. Attempts to disarm and demobilize them have been largely hampered by political indecisiveness and a culture of impunity institutionalized following the fall of Qaddafi's regime. The militia fighters received one payment ($3,140 for married and $1,884 for unmarried fighters) without having to provide substantial proof for their contribution or to return weapons. In May 2012, Law 38 granted them immunity for "military, security, or civilian acts undertaken with the aim of ensuring the revolution's success and its goal,"[30] including murder and forced displacement, seizure, detention, and interrogation of detainees outside a legal framework. The longer these militias existed outside any system of control or oversight, the more empowered they became. In the spring of 2013, they laid siege to the transitional parliament to coerce its members into voting for a somewhat controversial law banning anyone remotely linked to the Qaddafi regime from holding office. At the same time, Libya's oil output has decreased from 1.4 million barrels per day in early-2012 to 230,000, resulting in more than U.S.$10 billion losses.[31]

In Iraq, the previous militia problem of the early-2000s has been reduced, but it is still not entirely resolved. There are still a dozen militia groups in addition to three jihadi terrorist organizations. In contrast to these, the militias pursue a more political objective related to the future of Iraq, and employ territorial rather than asymmetric methods. In this, they challenge the state's security forces directly as they often pose as an alternative.

There are at least six Sunni militias, whose size and motivations have somewhat fluctuated over time (not including the three Jihadi organizations Al-Qaeda in Iraq, Ansar al-Islam and Ansar al-Sunna Sharia). The Sons of Iraq (also known as the Awakening Council, or Sahwa) have been coopted by the Iraqi government in the fight against al-Qaeda. They clashed again in 2013 in Anbar, along with other Sunni militias such as the Army of the Men of the Naqshbandi Order, the 1920 Revolution Brigade, the Islamic Army in Iraq, Hamas in Iraq, and the Mujahedeen Army.

On the Shiite end of the Iraqi spectrum, there are about the same number of groups showing the same degree of fluctuation. The Mahdi Army for instance, an armed group led by Muqtada al-Sadr, was formally disbanded in 2008 — only to be replaced by the Promised Day Brigades, whose size is estimated to be today at 5,000. Its one-time ally, the Asa'ib Ahl al-Haq (League of the Righteous), was created following a split with the Mahdi Army in 2006, and is believed to count about 2,000-3,000 men. The Kataib Hezbollah (not to be confused with the Lebanese Hezbollah) is a 400-man group and, like the others, enjoys considerable Iranian support. The Sheibani network, also known as the Kataib Sayyid al-Shuhada, counts about 200 men and is particularly experienced in smuggling. Most of the Badr Organization, related to the party Islamic Supreme Council of Iraq, has integrated into the Iraqi military, but remnants of it continue to be active outside the legal framework. All of these groups are rumored to be currently actively involved in the civil war in Syria on the side of the government.[32]

The same is true for the Lebanese Hezbollah; originally born in the context of the Israeli invasion of Lebanon in the early-1980s, it was exempted from the post-civil war demobilization of militias and continued as Lebanese resistance. It continued to launch attacks against Israel, resulting in a full scale war in 2006. Central governments are equally challenged in Yemen and, of course Syria, where paramilitary groups are seeking to topple the central government.

The disarmament, demobilization and reintegration (DDR) of these groups is more often than not part of a broader political problem rather than merely a technical process. In Lebanon, the disarmament of Hezbollah requires a broad societal consensus currently not in place; in Iraq, the multitude of militias reflects the inadequacy of the Iraqi state institutions as well as the discontent many Sunnis feel towards the post-Saddam Hussein system; in Libya, the central government is lacking the sheer capacity or legitimacy to disarm. Solving this issue therefore always requires a broad and holistic approach; political solutions hence have to precede the DDR process.

Lack of an Institutional Perception of the Need to Reform.

One of the main problems in Arab security sector reform is that the institutions themselves do not perceive the need for change. Resistance from within the bodies concerned makes reform attempts not only more difficult, it can derail the process altogether. Understanding the reasons for this resistance is important, as it provides the basis for strategies to counter it.

One reason for opposition to change is the fact that the delivery of security services in the countries concerned is satisfactory — or at least, used to be. Before the Arab Spring, homicide rates in Egypt were only a fifth of America's, and a 20th of Brazil's. The rationale for change is not always evident if the delivery of services seems adequate.

While this has changed since 2011 — in Egypt, homicide rates have tripled from 774 in 2010 to 2,144 in 2012[33] — Arab citizens are, across the board, satisfied with the security services they receive from their states, see Figure 1. According to a survey conducted in 12 Arab countries,[34] 67 percent of respondents were satisfied or somewhat satisfied with security in their home countries, with a great variety across countries. Overwhelming satisfaction — 90 percent — was reported in states such as Jordan, Saudi Arabia, and Mauritania; 60-75 percent satisfaction was recorded in Sudan, Lebanon, Egypt, Tunisia, and Palestine. Overall, numbers were less positive in states with regular political unrest; Iraqis for instance were overwhelmingly dissatisfied—57 percent—with their level of security.

DUE TO COPYRIGHT RESTRICTIONS
SOME OR ALL IMAGES ARE NOT INCLUDED

Source: United Nations Office on Drugs and Crime, available from *https://www.unodc.org/unodc/en/data-and-analysis/homicide.html.*

Figure 1. Intentional Homicide, Rate per 100,000 Population (1995-2011).

The institutions themselves fare surprisingly well; 77 percent of Arab citizens were confident or somewhat confident in their countries' armed forces—the highest level of trust any institution could gather. The police forces are deemed trustworthy or somewhat trustworthy according to 55 percent of respondents—in comparison, 47 percent are confident in government, 36 percent declare to have trust in their country's legislative body, and 23 percent in political parties.[35] Although it is true that the Arab Spring has challenged, in particular, the internal security forces, even at the height of anti-police sentiment in Egypt, 39 percent of respondents deemed the police forces to be very good or somewhat good.[36] The virtual self-destruction of the police forces in Egypt, for instance, has reminded the population of the importance of the police. The involvement of the security actors in question when attempting reform remains therefore crucial; in Egypt's new constitution, perhaps the most important novelty is that the police are now explicitly loyal to the people (Articles 206 and 207), echoing the military's mission. The document created a new institution, the Supreme Police Council, which is required to be consulted on any law which would affect the police. In practice, this means that police reform will always have to be conducted in close coordination with an element of the police itself.

In particular, the concept of accountability faces a lot of resistance. Following the indictment of Tunisia's chief of the intervention forces who was accused of having opened fire on protesters, the interior minister attempted to dismiss him. In response, thousands of police officers withdrew from their posts in strike, saying "we will not be the scapegoats for the families of the victims." The protesters succeeded in overturning the chief's dismissal, and he eventually was found not guilty. This is a trend which echoes through almost all Arab countries; police, and military officers generally are tried by military courts, not civilian ones, and are therefore removed from civilian measures of discipline. This does not necessarily imply that police officers on trial will automatically walk free—In Egypt, for example, First Lieutenant Mahmoud Sohby el-Shinnawy was convicted for 3 years for firing cartouche rounds at protesters in November 2011, while Mahmoud Salah Mahmoud and Awad Soliman, two police officers charged with the death of protester Khaled Said in 2010, were handed 10-year prison sentences — this is more often than not the case. On the other hand, none of the nine officers indicted in 2012 following riots at a soccer stadium that cost the lives of at least 74 people were sentenced.[37] Six officers charged in the context of the death of 83 protesters in Alexandria in 2011 were also acquitted.[38]

This culture of impunity does not help to institutionalize an atmosphere of reform, in which accountability plays a major role. In return, the aftermath of 2011 created the reverse situation in which security agents were considered guilty by association. In Tunisia, Libya, and Egypt, police stations were ransacked as symbols of the former regime; reform attempts in an environment which antagonized large parts of the existing security structure were met with resistance.

The key to overcoming institutional opposition to change can be approached with different strategies. Involving the security sector will lead not only to cooperation but also to a sense of ownership which is crucial to SSR success. Appealing to professional ethics and identity is equally bound to be more successful than patronizing civilian attitudes. Ultimately, SSR against the wishes of the sector in question will always result in mitigated success, if not to say failure.

Conclusion.

Arab security sectors, for better or for worse, remain one of the pillars of Arab states. Without security, no economic development is possible in either Libya or Egypt — economic conditions led to the 2011 events in the first place. Western governments so far have refrained from extensive SSR in the Arab world, preferring security sector assistance or occasional training. What 2011 has shown, however, is that reforms are not only beneficial, but at this stage mandatory. Since civilian actors are themselves challenged by ongoing transitions, the main agents in this reform will have to be the institutions themselves. Understanding their concerns and needs will certainly foster their cooperation — and, in any case, reform is crucial to deliver the efficient and legally bound security sector citizens and international supporters alike are striving for.

ENDNOTES

1. Florence Gaub, "Arab Armies: Agents of Change?" Chaillot Paper No. 131, Paris, France: European Union Institute for Security Studies, March 2014.

2. Risa A. Brooks, "Civil-Military Relations and Military Effectiveness: Egypt in the 1967 and 1973 Wars," Risa A. Brooks and Elizabeth A. Stanley, eds., *Creating Military Power: The Sources of Military Effectiveness*, Redwood City, CA: Stanford University Press, 2007.

3. Eliezer Be'eri, "The Waning of the Military Coup in Arab Politics," *Middle Eastern Studies*, Vol. 18, No. 1, January 1982, pp. 69-81.

4. William R. Thompson, "Toward Explaining Arab Military Coups," *Journal of Political and Military Sociology*, Vol. 2, Fall, 1974, pp. 237-250.

5. Brooks, pp. 106-134.

6. Florence Gaub, "The Libyan Armed Forces between Coup-proofing and Repression," *Journal of Strategic Studies*, Vol. 36, No. 2, April 1, 2013.

7. World Bank, *World Development Report 2011: Conflict, Security, and Development*, Washington, DC: The International Bank for Reconstruction and Development, 2011, p. 11.

8. "Military Retain 8-Year Veto over Defense Minister in Egypt's Constitution," *Alahram Online*, November 20, 2013, available from *english.ahram.org.eg/NewsContent/1/64/87088/Egypt/Politics-/Military-retain-year-veto-over-defence-minister-in.aspx*.

9. The Constitution of the Arab Republic of Egypt 2014, Article 203, available from *www.sis.gov.eg/Newvr/Dustor-en001.pdf*.

10. "GNC Empowers Abu Sahmain with 'Commander-in-Chief' Duties," *Libya Herald*, January 23, 2014, available from *www.libyaherald.com/2014/01/23/gnc-empowers-abu-sahmain-with-commander-in-chief-duties/#axzz2xH4EXEGK*.

11. "Libyan Rebel Leader Sacks Executive Branch of Transitional Council," *Al-Arabiya*, August 8, 2011, available from *english.alarabiya.net/articles/2011/08/08/161430.html*.

12. "840 Killed in Egypt's Revolution, Health Ministry Official Says," *Al-Masry Al-Youm*, April 4, 2011, available from *www.almasryalyoum.com/en/node/385973*.

13. Human Rights Watch, "Egypt: Retry or Free 12,000 after Unfair Military Trials," September 10, 2011, available from *https://www.hrw.org/news/2011/09/10/egypt-retry-or-free-12000-after-unfair-military-trials*.

14. Michele Dunne, "Egypt's Unprecedented Instability by the Numbers," Washington, DC: Carnegie Endowment for International Peace, March 24, 2014, available from *carnegieendowment.org/2014/03/24/egypt-s-unprecedented-instability-by-numbers/h5j3*.

15. Abo Elnnaga, Press Conference of the Egyptian Minister of the Interior, February, 19, 2013 (in Arabic).

16. "Egyptians Become Victims of Soaring Crime Rate," *Financial Times*, May 1, 2013, available from *www.ft.com/intl/cms/s/0/7ffac226-adab-11e2-a2c7-00144feabdc0.html#axzz2xWywGjZl*.

17. "Egyptian Police Go on Strike," *The Guardian*, March 10, 2013, available from *www.theguardian.com/world/2013/mar/10/egypt-police-strike*.

18. Florence Gaub, "A Libyan Recipe for Disaster," *Survival*, Vol. 56, No. 1, February-March 2014, pp. 101-120.

19. "Assassination Campaign Blights Eastern Libya," *Financial Times*, December 12, 2013, available from *www.ft.com/intl/cms/s/0/0e406cee-61ab-11e3-aa02-00144feabdc0.html#axzz2xWywGjZl*.

20. "Jihadist Group Claims Egypt Police General Killing," *Antaranews*, January 29, 2014, available from *www.antaranews.com/en/news/92424/jihadist-group-claims-egypt-police-general-killing*.

21. "One Dead, 529 Convicted: A Story of Judicial Revenge in Egypt," *The Christian Science Monitor*, March 28, 2014, available from *www.csmonitor.com/World/Middle-East/2014/0328/One-dead-529-convicted-a-story-of-judicial-revenge-in-Egypt*.

22. "In Libya, Militias Rule," *Al-Monitor*, June 18, 2013, available from *www.al-monitor.com/pulse/originals/2013/06/libya-intelligence-security-benghazi.html*.

23. *Stockholm International Peace Research Institute (SIPRI) Military Expenditure Database 1988-2012*, Stockholm, Sweden: SIPRI, available from *milexdata.sipri.org/files/?file=SIPRI+milex+data+1988-2012+v2.xlsx*.

24. "Tunisia Increases Defence Budget," *Magharebia*, November 6, 2013, available from *magharebia.com/en_GB/articles/awi/features/2013/11/06/feature-03*; "Interior Ministry's Budget Increases," *Daily News Egypt*, May 25, 2013, available from *www.dailynews-egypt.com/2013/05/25/interior-ministry-rep-asks-for-budget-raise/*.

25. "Egypt Boosts Police Salaries as Forces Join Mounting Strikes by Doctors, Textile Workers," Foxnews, February 19, 2014, available from *www.foxnews.com/world/2014/02/19/egypt-boosts-police-salaries-as-forces-join-mounting-strikes-by-doctors-textile/*.

26. *Lebanon: Improved Security Key to Growth Revival*, Washington, DC: Institute of International Finance, January 22, 2014, available from *www.iif.com/emr/resources+3312.php*.

27. World Economic Forum and the European Bank for Reconstruction and Development (EBRD), *The Arab World Competitiveness Report 2013*, World Economic Forum, Geneva, Switzerland, 2013, available from *www3.weforum.org/docs/WEF_AWCR_Report_2013.pdf*.

28. *Global Competitiveness Report 2013-2014*, World Economic Forum, Geneva, Switzerland, 2013, available from *www3.weforum.org/docs/WEF_GlobalCompetitivenessReport_2013-14.pdf*.

29. "Heavy Hand of the Secret Police Impeding Reform in Arab World," *The New York Times*, November 14, 2005, available from *www.nytimes.com/2005/11/14/international/middleeast/14jordan.html?pagewanted=all&_r=0*.

30. "Libya grants immunity to 'revolutionaries'," Air France Press, May 3, 2012, available from *www.alarabiya.net/articles/2012/05/03/211978.html*.

31. "Libya Oil Output Dives after Key Field Shut," *Aljazeera*, February 23, 2014, available from *www.aljazeera.com/news/africa/2014/02/libya-oil-output-dives-after-key-field-shut-2014223153123479374.html*.

32. Michael Knights, "Iran's Foreign Legion: The Role of Iraqi Shiite Militias in Syria," Washington, DC: The Washington Institute, June 27, 2013, available from *www.washingtoninstitute.org/policy-analysis/view/irans-foreign-legion-the-role-of-iraqi-shiite-militias-in-syria*; *Mapping Militant Organizations, Iraq*, Redwood, CA: Stanford University, available from *www.stanford.edu/group/mappingmilitants/cgi-bin/maps/view/iraq*.

33. "Egyptians Become Victims of Soaring Crime Rate."

34. Algeria, Egypt, Iraq, Jordan, Lebanon, Mauritania, Morocco, Palestine, Saudi Arabia, Sudan, Tunisia, and Yemen.

35. "The Arab Opinion Project: The Arab Opinion Index," Qatar: Arab Center for Research and Policy Studies, March 2012, p. 46, available from *english.dohainstitute.org/release/5083cf8e-38f8-4e4a-8bc5-fc91660608b0*.

36. "Egyptians Embrace Revolt Leaders, Religious Parties and Military, As Well," Pew Research Global Attitudes Project, April 25, 2011, available from *www.pewglobal.org/2011/04/25/egyptians-embrace-revolt-leaders-religious-parties-and-military-as-well/*.

37. "75 Charged in Deaths at Soccer Riot in Egypt," *The New York Times*, March 15, 2012, available from *www.nytimes.com/2012/03/16/world/middleeast/75-charged-in-deaths-at-soccer-riot-in-egypt.html?_r=0*.

38. "Verdict in Police Brutality Case in Egypt May Be Exception," *Al-Monitor*, March 4, 2014, available from *www.al-monitor.com/pulse/originals/2014/03/egypt-khaled-said-alexandria-trial-police-brutality.html#ixzz2zuLRhwEj*.

U.S. ARMY WAR COLLEGE

Major General William E. Rapp
Commandant

*****

STRATEGIC STUDIES INSTITUTE
and
U.S. ARMY WAR COLLEGE PRESS

Director
Professor Douglas C. Lovelace, Jr.

Director of Research
Dr. Steven K. Metz

Author
Dr. Florence Gaub

Editor for Production
Dr. James G. Pierce

Publications Assistant
Ms. Rita A. Rummel

*****

Composition
Mrs. Jennifer E. Nevil

www.ingramcontent.com/pod-product-compliance
Lightning Source LLC
Chambersburg PA
CBHW061805280526
45787CB00003BA/1489